I0160608

I LOVE LIFE!

I LOVE ME!

This Book Belongs to

I LOVE LIFE!

I LOVE ME!
How to Love Yourself and Others:
A Guide for Teens and Young Adults

I LOVE LIFE! I LOVE ME!

How to Love Yourself and Others:
A Guide for Teens and Young Adults

Anthony Dwane Parnell

Books by Anthony Parnell

www.LoveLifeLoveMe.com
www.LoveLifeLoveMeDay.com

I LOVE LIFE! I LOVE ME!
How to Love Yourself and Others:
A Guide for Teens and Young Adults

Copyright © 2018 Anthony Dwane Parnell

All rights reserved. No part of this publication may be reproduced, distributed, or transmitted in any form or by any means, including photocopying, recording, or other electronic or mechanical methods, without the prior written permission of the publisher, except in the case of brief quotations embodied in critical reviews and certain other noncommercial uses permitted by copyright law.

Books by Anthony Parnell
Las Vegas, Nevada

ISBN# 978-0-9644205-3-3

Library of Congress Control Number: 2018905863

Cover Photographs/Images Credits:

- ARochau/Adobe Stock (Zwei Kletterer im Klettersteig)

- Andrey Popov/Shutterstock

- Samuel Borges Photography/Shutterstock

- Elnur/Shutterstock

TABLE OF CONTENTS

CHAPTER ONE: Ten "Life Affirming Principles"   1

CHAPTER TWO: Self-Reflection and Journaling   17

CHAPTER THREE: Affirmations   43

CHAPTER FOUR: Incorporating Life Affirming
                    Principles into Your Daily Life   79

INTRODUCTION

TO THE STUDENTS:

My name is Anthony. I was inspired to write this book given the crisis surrounding teens and young adults in America. This includes increased incidences of suicide and gun violence. I have come to the conclusion that much of this stems from many teens and young adults not having a roadmap, a guide or clear answers for how to deal with their pain and suffering, their fear, their low sense of self-worth and their anxiety about what is to come in the future.

Not until recently did I realize why I've dedicated my life to understanding and finding solutions to helping youth cope with the societal pressures of adolescence and young adulthood. I, in fact, have spent nearly thirty years of my life and thousands of hours working with youth and their families in homes, schools, summer day camps and treatment centers facilitating individual and group counseling sessions to help young people feel their way out of the darkness. Now I know the answer to why I have been on this journey the last few decades of my life. It is because my very unique childhood experiences, between the years of twelve and eighteen, played a significant part in shaping who I have become and what I believe. It was during these years that seeds were planted and I unconsciously was pointed in the direction of working with youth and young adults. Why? To help them journey down a life path in which they not only find happiness but are able to reach their full potential.

The overall goal of this book is to encourage you to consistently practice thinking and feeling more positively about your life and yourself (in particular, your self-identity) and to develop a greater sense of confidence that you can accomplish your goals and become the person you want to be. This book and the life affirming principles I have shared in it are written for you. It is something I did not have. I hope it will help you in your personal journey. Or, if you have a friend who is searching for answers, doubting themselves and trying to find a reason to believe that life is worth living, I encourage you to share this book with them.

Finally, if this book speaks to you and sparks a feeling of hope, encouragement, and excitement, don't hesitate to reach out to me. I would be more than happy to join a kickoff for your "I LOVE LIFE! I LOVE ME!" DAY at your school or organization.

Wishing you much success and fulfillment in life!

Anthony Parnell, M.S.W.

TO THE ADMINISTRATORS:

Learning to love yourself, whether you're a teenager or an adult, is a treasured gift. This is particularly true at a time when we, in America, are bombarded with news clips of acts of violence on innocent people and a rising number of teenagers and young adults who are attempting and committing suicide. Thus, the need for more individuals to learn to love themselves is more important than ever.

There are countless stories of highly successful adults—mostly unnamed—who at one point in their lives seriously struggled with depression and/or emotional wounds from childhood traumas. Yet somehow, they were able to grab hold of a lifeline to pull themselves up. This book, then, is meant to serve as a lifeline for youth who are trying to develop a positive outlook on life and find a sense of purpose and meaning in their lives.

While many people choose to focus on the mounting death count of epidemics such as gun violence and suicide, this is a book that is intentionally meant to focus on life affirming principles, tools, and strategies for generating and sustaining positive energy in the lives of teens and young adults within our schools and within our broader communities. I, therefore, urge you to not just view *I Love Life! I Love Me! How to Love Yourself and Others: A Guide for Teens and Young Adults* as a book. Rather, also view it as a guide because the material is presented in a way that walks the reader through a step-by-step process of being introduced to life affirming principles and then challenging them to take an in-depth look at how these principles can be incorporated into their lives.

For teenagers who are struggling at school, at home, or in their peer relations, this is a method and approach that can be used to help them work through their inner conflicts, self-doubts and find resolution and clarity to many of life's questions. Equally important, the life principles, questions, and writing exercises presented in this guide lend themselves perfectly to facilitating meaningful dialogue among youth in formal group settings as well as in informal peer-to-peer settings.

Once again, given my extensive experience working with youth in a wide range of settings and helping them learn to navigate life's challenges, I am confident that this book offers meaningful content, as well as inspiration, that you and your students can pull from and immediately implement in your school or organization. I look forward to having the opportunity to work with you and your students as they learn to celebrate life and to celebrate themselves.

Thanks for caring! Thanks for supporting our youth!

Anthony Parnell, M.S.W.

www.LoveLifeLoveMe.com

www.LoveLifeLoveMeDay.com

CHAPTER ONE:

TEN "LIFE AFFIRMING PRINCIPLES"

LIFE PRINCIPLE #1
"Courage is fundamental in life."

Courage is a life skill that is needed to overcome adversity and many of life's challenges. When you are not feeling good about yourself and about your life, it takes courage to wake up every day with a positive mindset and a will to live. This is true whether you are dealing with challenges at home, at school or in your relationships with others (i.e. peer pressure).

A key building block to developing inner courage is first learning to be honest with yourself and with others about how you truly feel and what you really want out of life. This is a very important life lesson to learn because many youth and young adults live in the shadow of their parents and family's expectations. And, they feel too guilty **or/are** too afraid to share how they really feel and what direction is really important to them to take in their life.

LIFE PRINCIPLE #2:
"Feelings and Emotions are not bad."

Embrace and own your feelings instead of pushing them away. Because emotions are natural expressions and an indication that we are human and alive, we should never block them or try to hide from them. Instead, focus on finding a healthy outlet, especially with people who you fully trust to express and share your emotions with. The truth is, the longer you hold them inside, the greater the risk that your pent-up feelings and emotions will have a damaging effect on your mental, physical and emotional state.

LIFE PRINCIPLE #3:

"Questioning and Self-Exploration are essential ingredients for growing from youth to adulthood."

The growing pains we experience in life are not always physical. We also experience growing pains with how we view the world and how we view ourselves. And it is these changes in how we see things that often creates many of the insecurities and uncertainties that we feel.

Most of us have gone through similar inner struggles, questioning life and ourselves in an attempt to find answers to the meaning of life and why we are here. So, don't beat yourself up about it. Just know that, even though you might not be able to see it right now, there is a light at the end of the tunnel. Things will get better over time. You just have to be willing to keep moving forward with a positive attitude. Don't allow yourself to be stuck dwelling on the challenges and negative things you are experiencing in your life right now.

LIFE PRINCIPLE #4:

"Death and Dying are a part of life."

The longer we live the greater the probability that we will lose someone or something that means a lot to us. To get through the pain and the hurt of our loss, we have to remind ourselves there is no exact science that determines when we are born or when we die. Yet, while we are alive on this earth, what we do have control over is how we use our free will in deciding if we want to be creators of life or destroyers of life.

This is a very significant decision to make now in your life because, the longer you live, the more you will notice how certain people choose to have a more negative mindset and outlook on life than a positive mindset and outlook. The sad truth is, it is often much easier to destroy life than it is to create and preserve it; it is much easier to tear something or someone down than it is to build something or to lift someone up.

Throughout your life, you will constantly be tested and challenged as to whether or not you are able to maintain a mindset and approach to life that is focused on what is beautiful and great, and not what is ugly and wrong in the world. Therefore, it is highly important that you start surrounding yourself with like-minded and like-spirited people who are focused on life, not death; people who are focused on living life to the fullest and who are striving to create rather than destroy; people who are not wallowing in doom and gloom over the inevitable fact that one day we all will die.

LIFE PRINCIPLE #5
"Everyone and everything is interconnected."

Everything we say and do directly and indirectly affects everyone around us. This is because everyone and everything on the planet and in the universe is interconnected. This includes you! Take a moment and allow this to sink in: we are connected to everything, from the earth revolving around the sun to a tiny tree frog in the middle of the Amazon rain forest! And in everything we do – whether it's breathing air, drinking water or helping ourselves or a friend – we are either taking something from nature or those around us or adding to it.

The point I'm trying to make is that there are countless natural connections that automatically exist all around us every day in life whether or not we are aware of them and acknowledge and embrace them. However, I am a firm believer that when we do look for and fully embrace these natural connections, it makes us stronger and wiser. We feel happier, more alive, and we gain access to a wider support system and greater knowledge than we could ever possibly possess ourselves.

Everyone and everything in the universe
is interconnected.

The sun.
The moon.
The earth.
The heavens.
We are one.

And, just like a grain of sand on the beach
is merely a small particle of many particles,
we, too,
in our human existence
are merely a small atomic particle
in comparison to the whole.

We are created
and, we become creators.
Our lives are like the tree that has many branches,
we are connected to the roots
of the tree of life.

Anthony Parnell

LIFE PRINCIPLE #6

"Happiness and fulfillment begins with learning how to be grateful in each and every moment."

The greatest happiness and sense of fulfillment generally comes when we learn to be grateful with where we currently are in life. One way to practice this daily habit is to make sure you are celebrating and appreciating the smallest accomplishments and blessings in your daily life. Too often, we are so consumed with trying to accomplish our biggest goals that we forget that it is the little goals along the way that first must be accomplished.

Also, in spending so much time, energy and effort in trying to accomplish our biggest goals, we tend to get frustrated when we're not making progress as fast as we think we should. This is when we are most vulnerable to falling victim to having a mindset in which we are focusing more on problems than solutions. Sometimes, we also are so desperate to accomplish major goals in our life that we become impatient and start comparing our lives and what we tangibly have to what others around us have. But, if we stay focused on always making sure to celebrate the smallest things in life, our smallest accomplishments, it will be that much easier to maintain a mindset and attitude where we are constantly valuing, appreciating and finding contentment in what we do have and where we currently are in life. Otherwise, it is that much easier to become a prisoner to worry and concern about what we "do not have" and what is not working rather than what is working.

Let today be the day that you make the promise to yourself, that no matter how great the challenge that lies in front of you, you will always strive to be mindful of and grateful for all the things you currently do have in your life while patiently working towards acquiring the other things you desire in life.

LIFE PRINCIPLE #7
"True friends always wish the best for us."

Friendship is genuine and true friends always wish the best for us - even when personal loss or personal sacrifice is required of them. When we have the courage to surround ourselves with "true" friends, it is much easier to maintain a healthier sense of ourselves and develop emotional and spiritual strength to apply in our daily interactions.

Many times, we know deep inside that the individuals we call our friends are not "true friends." But, somehow, they became a part of our close circle for any number of reasons; they're popular, they look good or they're tough and other students don't mess with them! Basically, we feel protected by being associated with them.

You may not have discovered it yet, but you possess a special ingredient inside of you called "courage." It's inside of you because it is inside of everyone. If you haven't already discovered it, once you do you will find the courage to choose who your friends are based on a definition of "true friendship," rather than only allowing them to choose you as a friend.

LIFE PRINCIPLE #8
"There is power in our words and in our thoughts."

Our words and the words of others have the power to make us feel loved, to be inspired, and to feel hopeful about a better tomorrow or to feel completely bummed out! This is because the words we repeatedly speak and the thoughts we constantly focus on in our mind have positive energy and negative energy. Thus, the more we practice speaking positive words and thinking positive thoughts the more positive energy we are creating in our lives.

The more positive we think and feel the more confident we are in our ability to accomplish anything we desire. For example, someone telling you they love you or "that's a nice shirt you're wearing," can make your day. They just sent you positive energy, and it's likely to bring a smile to your face. Well, we can do the same for ourselves by consciously choosing to say positive things to ourselves and about ourselves. We also can purposely close our eyes and intentionally think positive thoughts rather than allowing negative thoughts to creep in and take over in our minds.

LIFE PRINCIPLE #9
"A hug sometimes can say more than words."

Every day, at schools across America, parents can be seen hugging their children as they send them off to school. This may sound like a simple thing, but for the child, it's a reminder that someone cares about them and is there to support them. And, for the parents, it also is their way of connecting with their kids. So, it can work both ways. The person initiating the hug gets as much reward as the person who is receiving the hug.

The reality, however, is that it's easy to hug someone when things are going great. It becomes more difficult when you can feel that someone you care about is struggling emotionally. This is because emotion and feelings make many people uncomfortable, even adults.

This is why, sometimes, you must take responsibility for telling the people you love, your parents in particular, "*I need a hug!*" Frequently, your parents and other adults who care about you may get scared or uncomfortable when dealing with the emotions of others, let alone their own emotions. Or, in some situations, they just are so busy juggling everything going on in their life that they are unaware of any intense emotions you might be feeling and are trying to deal with.

I want to encourage you to not drown out your feelings and emotions to the point that you can't tell the difference between being happy and sad or excited and angry. I'm saying this because I've seen it happen time and time again with many students. They've endured so many struggles that a part of them shuts down emotionally. And because they've been carrying around so much hurt, pain and confusion for so long, they are now living day-to-day in survival mode. They're physically alive but emotionally and spiritually dead.

Hopefully, you haven't become totally numb to everyone and everything around you. But, if you have, don't be afraid to admit to yourself and to those who love you that you need to talk and possibly that *you need a hug*!

LIFE PRINCIPLE #10:
"Love is a powerful and ever-present life force."

Love has the power to heal our wounds. Love has the power to make us whole again when we've been broken. Even when you are not feeling loved and it feels like your life is not worth living, there is always something good and positive to live for.

Love helps us cope with and overcome life's challenges. The more we love ourselves and the more we believe in ourselves, the easier it is to cope with and overcome life's challenges. Reciting daily affirmations and taking time each day to practice deep breathing, to sit in silence, and to journal are ways to become more at peace and more content with ourselves.

Before giving up on life, you can choose to challenge yourself to make sure you have tried your best to be open to receiving love from others and to practice loving yourself on a daily basis.

CHAPTER TWO:

SELF-REFLECTION AND JOURNALING

Now that you have been introduced to the "Ten Life Affirming Principles," I would like you to take some time to think about how strongly you believe in each of these life affirming principles. Also, consider 1) Are you currently using these life affirming principles in your life? 2) If so, in what ways can they begin to have a greater impact in your life? That is, how can they become a stronger influence in your life?

As a first step, review and complete the **LIFE AFFIRMING PRINCIPLES REPORT CARD (Self-Graded) on the following page.** Give yourself a grade in each of the ten principles. (A = highest score; F = lowest score)

A = Very Strong I do an amazing job of using this Principle regularly in my life.

B = Strong I do a good job of using this Principle in my life.

C = Average I have used this Principle a few times but still need to work on using it more.

D = Okay I only remember using this Principle once or twice in my life.

F = Needs a Lot of Work I do not remember ever using this Principle in my life.

Remember, there are no right or wrong answers. This is simply a measuring stick of your current view of life and yourself in relation to the Ten Life Affirming Principles.

Once you complete the Self-Graded Report Card, feel free to record any general thoughts and/or observations of how you see your life at this time. Use the "Notes" pages in the back of the book or use a separate piece of paper.

LIFE AFFIRMING PRINCIPLES REPORT CARD
(Self-Graded)

PRINCIPLES	Grade
PRINCIPLE #1: Courage is fundamental in life because it is a life skill that is needed to overcome adversity and many of life's challenges. "I have courage when dealing with conflict with others and with confronting and not avoiding life challenges at home and at school. I am practicing courage on a consistent basis."	
PRINCIPLE #2: Feelings and Emotions are not bad. "I accept and embrace my emotions without fear of what others think."	
PRINCIPLE #3: Questioning and Self-Exploration are essential ingredients in growing from youth to adulthood. "I don't feel guilty and am not afraid to ask questions about things that are very important to me in life."	
PRINCIPLE #4: Death and Dying are a part of life. "I allow myself to grieve and to feel and express my emotions about the people who meant a lot to me who have passed away."	
PRINCIPLE #5: Everyone and everything is interconnected. "I believe that everything I do and say directly and indirectly affects others."	
PRINCIPLE #6: Happiness and fulfillment begins with learning how to be grateful in each and every moment. "I am able to appreciate and celebrate the little things in life more than I focus on the negative things in life."	
PRINCIPLE #7: True friends always wish the best for us. "I have amazing friends and am strong enough to not allow someone to be my friend who brings trouble and harm my way and doesn't wish the best for me."	
PRINCIPLE #8: There is power in our words and in our thoughts. "I believe in the power of my words and my thoughts to be able to accomplish all of my life goals and to be happy and successful in life."	
PRINCIPLE #9: A hug sometimes can say more than words. "I am not afraid to ask family or friends for a hug when I need it."	
PRINCIPLE #10: Love is a powerful and ever-present life force. "I believe in the power of love to make my life better as well as the lives of others. I believe that I love myself as I should and that I am able to make the right decisions for myself because I love myself."	

Now that you have completed the Self-Graded Life Affirming Principles Report Card, it is much easier to pinpoint which principles you might want to prioritize and give the greatest amount of attention.

On the following pages, you can now begin to carefully think about each of the individual principles and how significant each one is to you at this point in your life.

So, let's move forward by spending some time focusing on each of the Life Affirming Principles one at a time!

PRINCIPLE #1:

"Courage is fundamental in life."

Courage is fundamental in life because it is a life skill that is needed to overcome adversity and many of life's challenges. The first step to developing courage is by always trying your best to confront life's challenges, at home and at school, rather than avoiding them.

REFLECTION on **PRINCIPLE #1:**

— What thought immediately came to mind when you read or heard this life principle? Does it trigger any emotions or feelings for you?

— Describe your most courageous act. How did that make you feel?

— What are you willing to do and work on to become stronger in this Life Principle?

PLEASE NOTE: You are invited to use this book as a workbook and write your REFLECTIONS directly on this page, OR get a separate journal or notebook for writing.

PRINCIPLE #2:

"Feelings and Emotions are not bad."

I accept and embrace my emotions without fear of what others think.

REFLECTION on **PRINCIPLE** #2:

— What thought immediately came to mind when you read or heard this life principle? Does it trigger any emotions or feelings for you?

— What are some feelings that you try to avoid or shy away from? Why do you think that is?

— What are you willing to do and work on to become stronger in this Life Principle?

PRINCIPLE #3:

"Questioning and Self-Exploration are essential ingredients in growing from youth to adulthood."

I don't feel guilty and am not afraid to ask questions about things that are very important to me in life.

REFLECTION on **PRINCIPLE #3:**

– What thought immediately came to mind when you read or heard this life principle? Does it trigger any emotions or feelings for you?

– What is the biggest question you have about life right now? Have you asked anyone about it? If not, who could you ask?

– What are you willing to do and work on to become stronger in this Life Principle?

PRINCIPLE #4:

"Death and Dying are a part of life."

I allow myself to grieve and to feel and express my emotions about the people who meant a lot to me who have passed away.

REFLECTION on PRINCIPLE #4:

- What thought immediately came to mind when you read or heard this life principle? Does it trigger any emotions or feelings for you?

- How do you create life? How can you commit to being a creator of life even when you are not feeling your best?

- What are you willing to do and work on to become stronger in this Life Principle?

PRINCIPLE #5:

"Everyone and everything is interconnected."

I believe everything I do and say directly and indirectly affects others.

REFLECTION on **PRINCIPLE** # 5:

— What thought immediately came to mind when you read or heard this life principle? Does it trigger any emotions or feelings for you?

— Describe a connection that has made you stronger and wiser.

— What are you willing to do and work on to become stronger in this Life Principle?

PRINCIPLE #6:

"Happiness and fulfillment begins with learning how to be grateful in each and every moment."

I can appreciate and celebrate the little things in life more than I focus on the negative things in life.

REFLECTION on **PRINCIPLE #6:**

– What thought immediately came to mind when you read or heard this life principle? Does it trigger any emotions or feelings for you?

– What is one intangible thing you are grateful for? Examples include things like talents, attributes, or faith.

– What are you willing to do and work on to become stronger in this Life Principle?

PRINCIPLE #7:

"True friends always wish the best for us."

I have amazing friends and am strong enough to not allow someone to be my friend who brings trouble and harm my way and doesn't wish the best for me.

REFLECTION on **PRINCIPLE #7:**

- What thought immediately came to mind when you read or heard this life principle? Does it trigger any emotions or feelings for you?

- Are you a true friend? How do you know?

- What are you willing to do and work on to become stronger in this Life Principle?

PRINCIPLE #8:

"There is power in our words and in our thoughts."

I believe in the power of my words and my thoughts to be able to accomplish all of my life goals and to be happy and successful in life.

REFLECTION on **PRINCIPLE #8:**

– What thought immediately came to mind when you read or heard this life principle? Does it trigger any emotions or feelings for you?

– How often do you compliment others? How do you feel when you give a compliment?

– What are you willing to do and work on to become stronger in this Life Principle?

PRINCIPLE #9

"A hug sometimes can say more than words."

I am not afraid to ask family or friends for a hug when I need it.

REFLECTION on **PRINCIPLE #9**

— What thought immediately came to mind when you read or heard this life principle? Does it trigger any emotions or feelings for you?

— Who is the best hugger you know? Why?

— What are you willing to do and work on to become stronger in this Life Principle?

PRINCIPLE #10:

"Love is a powerful and ever-present life force."

I believe in the power of love to make my life better as well as the lives of others. I believe that I love myself as I should and that I am able to make the right decisions for myself because I love myself.

REFLECTION on **PRINCIPLE #10:**

- What thought immediately came to mind when you read or heard this life principle? Does it trigger any emotions or feelings for you?

- How do you define love? What is the best example of love you have experienced or witnessed in your life?

- What are you willing to do and work on to become stronger in this Life Principle?

CHAPTER THREE:

AFFIRMATIONS

af·fir·ma·tion
[af-er-mey-sh*uh*n]

noun

1. positive words, thoughts, images and feelings upon which an individual focuses his or her attention.

2. the act of using the power of faith (belief) to maintain a positive state and to create positive life events.

3. statements of truth.

AFFIRMATIONS

The goal of this chapter is to introduce you to the concept of affirmations, that is, the practice of using specific written or recited statements that address something you greatly desire to achieve or to have unfold in your life. For example, you may want to get better grades, have more friends or make the basketball team.

As I stated in the introduction, the goal of this book is to encourage you to consistently practice thinking and feeling more positively about your life and yourself (in particular, your self-identity*) and to develop a greater sense of confidence that you can accomplish your goals and become the person you want to be. And, one way to do this is by utilizing the simple but effective tool of daily affirmations. This is a critical point to make because, due to complex patterns in our modern-day lifestyles, we are all highly prone to dwell on negative thoughts — to focus more on the problems and what is wrong in our life — rather than focus our attention on all the good things and what is going right in our lives. The good news is that, just as we have been programmed to think negatively, we also can be reprogrammed to think positively! Learning to use affirmations as a tool for how to think more positively is something that you can easily start practicing today at home, at school and all areas of your life.

As a starter exercise, first take some time to think of and write some simple "I LOVE LIFE" and "I LOVE ME" affirmation statements. Some examples have been provided to help get you started.

---

* See p.52 for definition of *self-identity*

"I LOVE LIFE" because.....

SAMPLE AFFIRMATIONS:

- I am glad to be alive and in good health.

- I have loving friends and family.

- I am able to enjoy things like being in the sun at the beach.

WRITE YOUR
"I LOVE LIFE" because.....
AFFIRMATIONS

1) I Love Life because......

2) I Love Life because......

3) I Love Life because......

4) I Love Life because......

PLEASE NOTE: You are invited to use this book as a workbook and write your AFFIRMATIONS directly on this page, OR get a separate journal or notebook for writing and keeping your AFFIRMATIONS.

"I LOVE ME" because.....

- I am smart and beautiful.

- I am a leader and care about people. I like to help people.

- I am really good at art.

WRITE YOUR
"I LOVE ME" because.....
AFFIRMATIONS

1) I Love Me because......

2) I Love Me because......

3) I Love Me because......

4) I Love Life Me because......

FOUR LIFE DOMAINS

Before moving on to writing additional AFFIRMATIONS, I first want to introduce you to the concept of Life Domains.

The Ten Life Affirming Principles can be applied to many areas of your life. However, I believe it is especially important for us to focus on four primary areas of your life or what I like to refer to as "Four Life Domains": Self-Identity; Peer Relations; School; Home (and Community).

FOUR LIFE DOMAINS	
Self-Identity	Peer Relations
School	Home (and Community)

Here are some short and simple definitions of each of the Domains:

Self-Identity – your overall view of yourself including both positive and negative perceptions; how you feel about your physical appearance and your academic, athletic and/or social abilities; your ability to love yourself and feel good about who you are; your self-esteem and the degree of confidence you feel in regard to accomplishing your goals and becoming the person you want to be.

Peer Relations – your ability to develop and maintain positive and healthy relationships with other youth and students in your neighborhood, community and school environment. This includes your ability to develop and maintain short-term as well as long-term friendships at school and at home that are mutually beneficial; your ability to utilize healthy and effective social skills such as teamwork and play in your interactions with friends and peers; your ability to communicate clearly, confidently, calmly and respectfully to adults and youth (i.e. the ability to use assertive communication rather than aggressive or passive communication).

School – your ability to perform well academically and achieve good grades as well as how you behave in a school setting; School behavior includes how well you are able to develop and maintain positive relationships with teachers/staff and other students that you interact with regularly in your learning environment.

Home (and Community) – your interactions with your family and all the people in your household; how you are maintaining your physical environment and relationships at home and in the broader community.

Now that you've had some practice writing affirmation statements and have been introduced to the concept of Four Life Domains, let's spend some time thinking about Affirmations you can write that specifically relate to each of the four life domains.

AFFIRMATIONS
for each of the
Four Life Domains

Self-Identity Affirmations

SAMPLE AFFIRMATIONS:

> ➤ I love myself and who I am the way I am.
> ➤ Day-by-day, I am becoming a stronger, wiser, and more confident person.

WRITE YOUR AFFIRMATIONS

1)

2)

Peer Relations Affirmations

SAMPLE AFFIRMATIONS:

➤ I have true friends at school who I can play with, talk to and always trust.

WRITE YOUR AFFIRMATIONS

1)

2)

School Affirmations

SAMPLE AFFIRMATIONS:

- ➤ I try my best at school by making sure I turn in all my assignments on-time.
- ➤ I don't beat myself up or get down on myself when I have a low grade or score on a test or assignment.
- ➤ I think positively and focus on learning each day and asking for help when I need it.

WRITE YOUR AFFIRMATIONS

1)

2)

Home (and Community) Affirmations

SAMPLE AFFIRMATIONS:

> ➤ I share my feelings with my parents and they listen, understand and don't judge me.

WRITE YOUR AFFIRMATIONS

1)

2)

AFFIRMATIONS

for each of the
LIFE AFFIRMING
PRINCIPLES

Dear Reader, if you've completed all the writing exercises in the previous sections, you should be proud of your emerging skill to write AFFIRMATIONS! Now you're ready to apply that skill again as you take a deeper look at yourself in relation to the Ten Life Affirming Principles. In the last writing exercise, you will write AFFIRMATIONS for each Life Affirming Principle. To help yourself, you can ask questions such as:

- What do I really believe about this Life Principle?

- How does this Life Principle fit into my life?

- How can this Life Principle become more active, effective or more powerful for me in my life?

WRITE YOUR AFFIRMATION for

PRINCIPLE #1:
"Courage is fundamental in life."

WRITE YOUR AFFIRMATION for

PRINCIPLE #2:
"Feelings and emotions are not bad."

WRITE YOUR AFFIRMATION for

PRINCIPLE #3:
"Questioning and Self-Exploration are essential ingredients in growing from youth to adulthood."

WRITE YOUR AFFIRMATION for

PRINCIPLE #4:
"Death and Dying are a part of life."

WRITE YOUR AFFIRMATION for

PRINCIPLE #5:
"Everyone and everything is interconnected."

WRITE YOUR AFFIRMATION for

PRINCIPLE #6:
"Happiness and fulfillment begins with learning how to be grateful in each and every moment."

WRITE YOUR AFFIRMATION for

PRINCIPLE #7:
"True friends always wish the best for us."

WRITE YOUR AFFIRMATION for

PRINCIPLE #8:
"There is power in our words and in our thoughts."

WRITE YOUR AFFIRMATION for

PRINCIPLE #9:
"A hug sometimes can say more than words."

WRITE YOUR AFFIRMATION for

PRINCIPLE #10:
"Love is a powerful and ever-present life force."

TAKE SMALL STEPS

Now that you have taken time to think about and write AFFIRMATIONS for each of the Four Life Domains and the Ten Life Affirming Principles, you can decide which one is most important to you to improve on or accomplish as soon as possible. As a reminder, in deciding which AFFIRMATION or goal you want to focus on right now in your life, it is recommended that you refer to the Self-Graded Report Card you completed in Chapter 2.

PRIORITY # 1   =   _____

_____

PRIORITY # 2   =   _____

_____

PRIORITY # 3   =   _____

_____

PRIORITY # 4   =   _____

Focusing initially on one Affirmation is important because it will allow you to build your confidence by seeing some level of progress or accomplishment with your goal. In other words, don't put too much pressure on yourself by trying to do too much too soon. The process of reprogramming your thoughts and feelings to be more positive can sometimes be slow, taking days, weeks or even months. More importantly, it requires daily discipline. So, start small and be consistent in the little things.

Literally write out your most important affirmation so that you can see it on a piece of paper or on the memo pad of your cell phone or in a Google doc. Then, memorize it and start reciting it out loud when you wake up in the morning, before you go to bed and anytime you are not feeling confident or strong in your ability to accomplish your goal. Reading your affirmations out loud may sound corny or weird, but believe me, it works. Just give it a try for at least a week and I'm confident you'll start to feel better; You'll feel a stronger sense of belief that you can accomplish any life goal you set your mind to accomplish.

An additional tool that can help you make sure you're taking small steps, instead of big steps (too soon), is writing out each of the small, baby steps that you will take in the beginning. Start by writing what you will do today, then what you will do tomorrow, this week, this month and so on. This approach can be very helpful in making sure you stay focused on taking things one day at time so that you can gradually build up to taking on more than one goal or even bigger goals that are much harder to accomplish.

TODAY

I will. . . . . .

_____

_____

_____

_____

_____

TOMORROW

I will. . . . . .

_____

_____

_____

_____

THIS WEEK

I will. . . . . .

_____

_____

_____

_____

_____

THIS MONTH
I will . . . .

_____

_____

_____

_____

_____

CHAPTER FOUR:

INCORPORATING LIFE AFFIRMING PRINCIPLES INTO YOUR DAILY LIFE

In this final chapter of the book, I simply want to introduce you to some activities that you can participate in as a way of helping you maintain a positive attitude about life and about yourself. In addition to participating in any of these recommended activities, always feel free to refer to any of the Ten Life Affirming Principles, the Four Life Domains, the AFFIRMATIONS you've written or any other section in this book to help you with any life challenge you are experiencing or any goal you are trying to accomplish.

ACTIVITY #1:

Join the
"I LOVE LIFE! I LOVE ME!"
Online Community

Finding ways to express yourself and to connect socially are important forms of communication for youth and adults. The "I LOVE LIFE! I LOVE ME!" Online Community provides a healthy outlet and opportunity for young people such as yourself to share and receive inspiration from other youth of their positive life experiences with celebrating life and celebrating themselves. It is a community where you can upload and view inspirational videos where you share "Life Affirming" projects you have created personally or as part of "I LOVE LIFE! I LOVE ME!" DAY at your school.

Visit www.LoveLifeLoveMe.com

ACTIVITY #2:

Join or Start
a Peer Support Group
at your school or in
your community

The Ten Life Affirming Principles were specifically developed with a group facilitation model in mind. They provide an excellent starting point when young people gather in small groups to talk through life challenges, and equally important, to encourage the development and continuation of peer support groups that are easily accessible and consistently available.

ACTIVITY #3:

Promote and Participate in
"I LOVE LIFE! I LOVE ME!" DAY
at your school
(or community organization)

VISIT: www.LoveLifeLoveMeDay.com

SUMMARY of
"I LOVE LIFE! I LOVE ME!" DAY

SCHOOLS (AND ORGANIZATIONS) NATIONWIDE ARE ENCOURAGED TO "CELEBRATE LIFE" by organizing and promoting "I LOVE LIFE! I LOVE ME!" DAY on their campus (or in their community). "I LOVE LIFE! I LOVE ME!" DAY can be a school-wide (or community-wide), day-long event where students celebrate things about life as well as celebrate things about themselves. The primary objective is to promote more positive energy and positive interactions among students on campus (and in our communities).

Much like a science fair, but not necessarily as elaborate, students have a variety of options for the type of project or format they can use to express themselves. They, for example, can write a narrative style essay, poem or journal entry. Or, they can create a song, skit or visual display such as artwork, a painting, or a poster. Most importantly, the students project must include a minimum of **"4 Things I Love About Life"**; and, a minimum of **"4 Things I Love about Me."**

The 1-Week Celebration culminates with a day for students to present and display the projects they have worked on.

VISIT www.**LoveLifeLovemeDay.com**

for more information on how your school or organization can organize
and promote "I LOVE LIFE! I LOVE ME!" DAY
on your campus.

Notes

Notes

Notes

Notes

Notes

Notes

www.ingramcontent.com/pod-product-compliance
Lightning Source LLC
Chambersburg PA
CBHW021344090426
42742CB00008B/737